What Animals Eat

CARNIVORES

James Benefield

raintree

a Capstone company — publishers for children

Raintree is an imprint of Capstone Global Library Limited, a company incorporated in England and Wales having its registered office at 7 Pilgrim Street, London, EC4V 6LB – Registered company number: 6695582

www.raintree.co.uk
myorders@raintree.co.uk

Edited by James Benefield and Amanda Robbins
Designed by Richard Parker
Picture research by Svetlana Zhurkin
Production by Helen McCreath
Originated by Capstone Global Library Ltd
Printed and bound in China

ISBN 978 1 4062 8910 7
18 17 16 15 14
10 9 8 7 6 5 4 3 2 1

British Library Cataloguing in Publication Data
A full catalogue record for this book is available from the British Library.

Acknowledgements
We would like to thank the following for permission to reproduce photographs:
Alamy: Martin Harvey, cover; Dreamstime: Vito Werner, 21; FLPA: Edward Myles, 14; Getty Images: Dr. Paul Zahl, 20; iStockphotos: Cristian Baitg, 4; Newscom: Universal Images Group/Dorling Kindersley, 23 (plankton); Shutterstock: Alan Jeffery, back cover (right), 19, Audrey Snider-Bell, 23 (spider), Brian Dunne, 17, 23 (mouse), Cathy Keifer, 13, Christian Schoissingeyer, 6, Dulce Rubia, 5, Gualtiero, 9, 23 (hyena), Heiko Kiera, 7, Holly Kuchera, 18, Mark Bridger, 11, Michael Rothschild, 15, Pavel K (footprints), throughout, photka, 16, Shackleford-Photography (hawk), back cover, 23, Stuart G. Porter, 8, 10, tolmachevr, 12, Yuriy Zhuravov, 23 (cows).

Every effort has been made to contact copyright holders of material reproduced in this book. Any omissions will be rectified in subsequent printings if notice is given to the publisher.

Disclaimer
All the internet addresses (URLs) given in this book were valid at the time of going to press. However, due to the dynamic nature of the internet, some addresses may have changed, or sites may have changed or ceased to exist since publication. While the author and publisher regret any inconvenience this may cause readers, no responsibility for any such changes can be accepted by either the author or the publisher.

Contents

Some words are shown in bold, **like this**.
You can find them in the glossary on page 23.

What do animals eat?

You need to eat the right food to live and grow. Animals need the right food, too. Different animals eat different things.

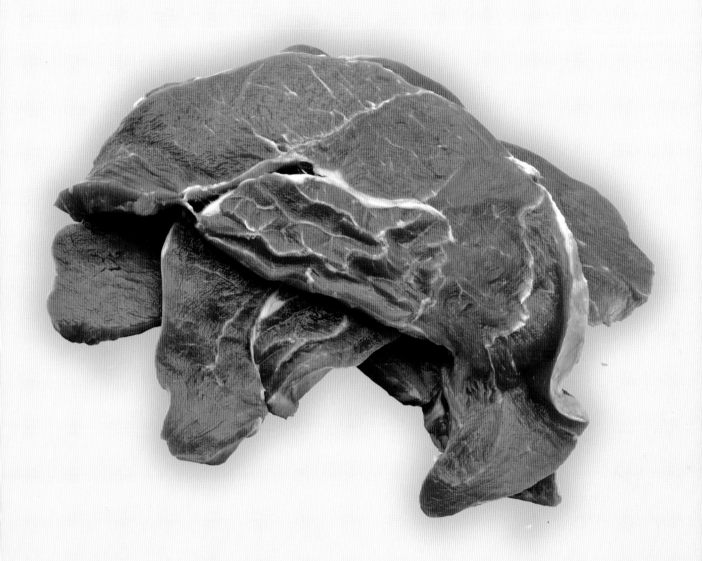

Carnivores are animals that usually eat meat.
Herbivores eat plants. Omnivores eat both
meat and plants.

What is a carnivore?

Carnivores eat all kinds of animals, from birds, to **rodents**, to fish. This otter is a carnivore and eats fish.

Some carnivores eat other carnivores. For example, a king cobra snake mainly eats other snakes.

Do all carnivores kill their food?

Carnivores who hunt other animals are called predators. The animals they hunt are called prey. Which animal is the predator in this picture?

Some carnivores don't always kill their food. They eat animals that have already died. These animals are called **scavengers**. A hyena is both a scavenger and a predator.

How do carnivores get food?

Carnivores often have large, strong jaws for grabbing prey. Look at the huge jaws this crocodile has!

Many carnivores have eyes on the front of their faces, such as this snow leopard. This helps them to see how far away their prey is.

How do carnivores eat food?

Many carnivores have special teeth for eating meat. Some of a polar bear's teeth are sharp. These teeth help it to grab and slice food.

Spiders are carnivores but some spiders have
no teeth. They kill their food with **venom**.
Then, they turn harder food into something
they can drink.

Carnivores all around

Some carnivores are in the air. A hawk is a **bird of prey**. It hunts small animals and sometimes snakes!

The sea is home to many kinds of carnivores.
For example, sharks are fish that are carnivores.
They eat smaller fish.

Can you find a carnivore in your home?

You, your family and friends might live with carnivores. We feed dogs special meaty food to keep them healthy.

We also feed cats special meaty food. But sometimes they bring home extra treats, such as mice.

Carnivores and people

In the United States, bobcats come into towns to get food from people's bins. Some people think bobcats are pests.

Sometimes, people kill carnivores that cause them problems. In some places, wolves eat **livestock**. Some farmers kill those wolves.

Strange carnivores

Fish that live in the deep sea can look very strange. These fish also eat special food. Lantern fish eat tiny creatures found in **plankton**.

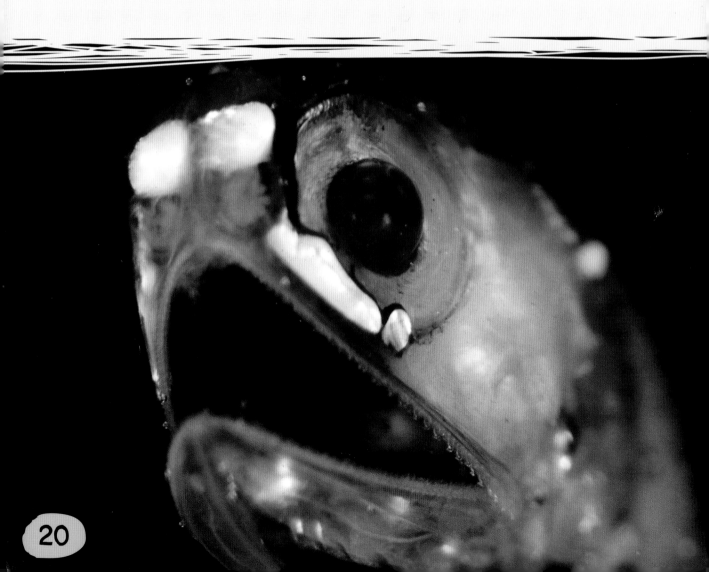

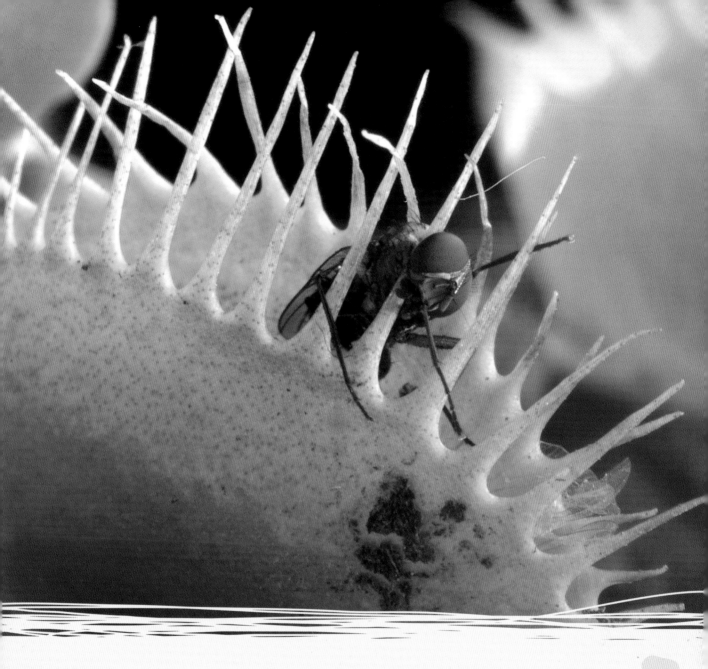

It's not just animals that eat other animals – just look at this picture! The Venus flytrap is a plant that eats insects.

Did you know?

- The blue whale is the world's largest carnivore and also the biggest animal on Earth. It is as long as three buses! Its food includes small sea animals called krill.

- The largest carnivore that lives on the land is the polar bear. They look cute but they are heavy. Polar bears can weigh 500 kg (over 1100 lb). That's the same as almost 100 cats!

- Some carnivores like to eat special meaty foods. Many snakes eat lots of animal eggs. Some snakes can live without eating food for a few months.

- We might love burgers and sausages, but we can't just eat meat. We also need to eat plenty of fruit and vegetables.

Picture glossary

bird of prey
large bird that kills animals

livestock
animals kept on farms, such as cows

plankton
small plant-like living things or animals
that float in the sea

rodent
small animals with big teeth, such
as mice

scavenger
animal that eats things that are
already dead

venom
special liquid that kills something.
It can be found in a spider's bite.

Find out more

Books

Carnivores, Aaron Reynolds (Chronicle Books, 2013)
Food Chain, M.P. Robertson (Frances Lincoln, 2012)

Website

resources.woodlands-junior.kent.sch.uk/revision/science/ foodchains.htm
This site explains why animals eat different things.

Index